MARTIN GUERRE

by

Alexandre Dumas

Copyright © 2012 Read Books Ltd.
This book is copyright and may not be
reproduced or copied in any way without
the express permission of the publisher in writing

British Library Cataloguing-in-Publication Data
A catalogue record for this book is available from the
British Library

Alexandre Dumas

Alexandre Dumas was born in Villers-Cotterêts, France in 1802. His parents were poor, but their heritage and good reputation – Alexandre's father had been a general in Napoleon's army – provided Alexandre with opportunities for good employment. In 1822, Dumas moved to Paris to work for future king Louis Philippe I in the Palais Royal. It was here that he began to write for magazines and the theatre.

In 1829 and 1830 respectively, Dumas produced the plays Henry III and His Court and Christine, both of which met with critical acclaim and financial success. As a result, he was able to commit himself full-time to writing. Despite the turbulent economic times which followed the Revolution of 1830, Dumas turned out to have something of an entrepreneurial streak, and did well for himself in this decade. He founded a production studio that turned out hundreds of stories under his creative direction, and began to produce serialised novels for newspapers which were widely read by the French public. It was over the next two decades, as a now famous and much loved author of romantic and adventuring sagas, that Dumas produced his best-known works – the D'Artagnan romances, including The Three Musketeers, in 1844, and The Count of Monte Cristo, in 1846.

Dumas made a lot of money from his writing, but he was almost constantly penniless as a result of his extravagant lifestyle and love of women. In 1851 he fled his creditors to Belgium, and then Russia, and then Italy, not returning to Paris until 1864. Dumas died in Puys, France, in 1870, at the age of 68. He is now enshrined in the Panthéon of Paris alongside fellow authors Victor Hugo and Emile Zola. Since his death, his fiction has been translated into almost a hundred languages, and has formed the basis for more than 200 motion pictures.

MARTIN GUERRE

We are sometimes astonished at the striking resemblance existing between two persons who are absolute strangers to each other, but in fact it is the opposite which ought to surprise us. Indeed, why should we not rather admire a Creative Power so infinite in its variety that it never ceases to produce entirely different combinations with precisely the same elements? The more one considers this prodigious versatility of form, the more overwhelming it appears.

To begin with, each nation has its own distinct and characteristic type, separating it from other races of men. Thus there are the English, Spanish, German, or Slavonic types; again, in each nation we find families distinguished from each other by less general but still well-pronounced features; and lastly, the individuals of each family, differing again in more or less marked gradations. What a multitude of physiognomies! What variety of impression from the innumerable stamps of the human countenance! What millions of models and no copies! Considering this ever changing spectacle, which ought to inspire us with most astonishment—the perpetual difference of faces or the accidental resemblance of a few individuals? Is it impossible that in the whole wide world there should be found by chance two people whose features are cast in one and the same mould? Certainly not; therefore that which ought to surprise us is not that these duplicates exist here and there upon the earth, but that they are to be met with in the same place, and appear together before our eyes, little accustomed to see such resemblances. From Amphitryon down to our own days, many fables have owed their origin to this fact, and history also has provided a few examples, such as the false Demetrius in Russia, the English Perkin Warbeck, and several other celebrated impostors, whilst the story we now present to our readers is no less curious and strange.

On the 10th of, August 1557, an inauspicious day in the history of France, the roar of cannon was still heard at six in the evening in the plains of St. Quentin; where the French army had just been destroyed by the united troops of England and Spain, commanded by the famous Captain Emanuel Philibert, Duke of Savoy. An utterly beaten infantry, the Constable Montmorency and several generals taken prisoner, the Duke d'Enghien mortally wounded, the flower of the nobility cut down like grass,—such were the terrible results of a battle which plunged France into mourning, and which would have been a blot on the reign of Henry II, had not the Duke of Guise obtained a brilliant revenge the following year.

In a little village less than a mile from the field of battle were to be heard the groans of the wounded and dying, who had been carried thither from the field of battle. The inhabitants had given up their houses to be used as hospitals, and two or three barber surgeons went hither and thither, hastily ordering operations which they left to their assistants, and driving out fugitives who had contrived to accompany the wounded under pretence of assisting friends or near relations. They had already expelled a good number of these poor fellows, when, opening the door of a small room, they found a soldier soaked in blood lying on a rough mat, and another soldier apparently attending on him with the utmost care.

"Who are you?" said one of the surgeons to the sufferer. "I don't think you belong to our French troops."

"Help!" cried the soldier, "only help me! and may God bless you for it!"

"From the colour of that tunic," remarked the other surgeon, "I should wager the rascal belongs to some Spanish gentleman. By what blunder was he brought here?"

"For pity's sake!" murmured the poor fellow, "I am in such pain."

"Die, wretch!" responded the last speaker, pushing him with his foot. "Die, like the dog you are!"

But this brutality, answered as it was by an agonised groan, disgusted the other surgeon.

"After all, he is a man, and a wounded man who implores help. Leave him to me, Rene."

Rene went out grumbling, and the one who remained proceeded to examine the wound. A terrible arquebus-shot had passed through the leg, shattering the bone: amputation was absolutely necessary.

Before proceeding to the operation, the surgeon turned to the other soldier, who had retired into the darkest corner of the room.

"And you, who may you be?" he asked.

The man replied by coming forward into the light: no other answer was needed. He resembled his companion so closely that no one could doubt they were brothers-twin brothers, probably. Both were above middle height; both had olive-brown complexions, black eyes, hooked noses, pointed chins, a slightly projecting lower lip; both were round-shouldered, though this defect did not amount to disfigurement: the whole personality suggested strength, and was not destitute of masculine beauty. So strong a likeness is hardly ever seen; even their ages appeared to agree, for one would not have supposed either to be more than thirty-two; and the only difference noticeable, besides the pale countenance of the wounded man, was that he was thin as compared with the moderate fleshiness of the other, also that he had a large scar over the right eyebrow.

"Look well after your brother's soul," said the surgeon to the soldier, who remained standing; "if it is in no better case than his body, it is much to be pitied."

"Is there no hope?" inquired the Sosia of the wounded man.

"The wound is too large and too deep," replied the man of science, "to be cauterised with boiling oil, according to the ancient method. 'Delenda est causa mali,' the source of evil must be destroyed, as says the learned Ambrose Pare; I ought therefore 'secareferro,'—that is to say, take off the leg. May God grant that he survive the operation!"

While seeking his instruments, he looked the supposed brother full in the face, and added—

"But how is it that you are carrying muskets in opposing armies, for I see that you belong to us, while this poor fellow wears Spanish uniform?"

"Oh, that would be a long story to tell," replied the soldier, shaking his head. "As for me, I followed the career which was open to me, and took service of my own free will under the banner of our lord king, Henry II. This man, whom you rightly suppose to be my brother, was born in Biscay, and became attached to the household of the Cardinal of Burgos, and afterwards to the cardinal's brother, whom he was obliged to follow to the war. I recognised him on the battle-field just as he fell; I dragged him out of a heap of dead, and brought him here."

During his recital this individual's features betrayed considerable agitation, but the surgeon did not heed it. Not finding some necessary instruments, "My colleague," he exclaimed, "must have carried them off. He constantly does this, out of jealousy of my reputation; but I will be even with him yet! Such splendid instruments! They will almost work of themselves, and are capable of imparting some skill even to him, dunce as he is!... I shall be back in an hour or two; he must rest, sleep, have nothing to excite him, nothing to inflame the wound; and when the operation is well over, we shall see! May the Lord be gracious to him!"

Then he went to the door, leaving the poor wretch to the care of his supposed brother.

"My God!" he added, shaking his head, "if he survive, it will be by the help of a miracle."

Scarcely had he left the room, when the unwounded soldier carefully examined the features of the wounded one.

"Yes," he murmured between his teeth, "they were right in saying that my exact double was to be found in the hostile army.... Truly one would not know us apart!... I might be surveying myself in a mirror. I did well to look for him in the rear of the Spanish army, and, thanks to the fellow who rolled him over so conveniently with that arquebus-shot; I was able to escape the dangers of the melee by carrying him out of it."

"But that's not all," he thought, still carefully studying the tortured face of the unhappy sufferer; "it is not enough to have got out of that. I have absolutely nothing in the world, no home, no resources. Beggar by birth, adventurer by fortune, I have enlisted, and have consumed my pay; I hoped for plunder, and here we are in full flight! What am I to do? Go and drown myself? No, certainly a cannon-ball would be as good as that. But can't I profit by this chance, and obtain a decent position by turning to my own advantage this curious resemblance, and making some use of this man whom Fate has thrown in my way, and who has but a short time to live?"

Arguing thus, he bent over the prostrate man with a cynical laugh: one might have thought he was Satan watching the departure of a soul too utterly lost to escape him.

"Alas! alas!" cried the sufferer; "may God have mercy on me! I feel my end is near."

"Bah! comrade, drive away these dismal thoughts. Your leg pains you—well they will cut it off! Think only of the other one, and trust in Providence!"

"Water, a drop of water, for Heaven's sake!" The sufferer was in a high fever. The would-be nurse looked round and saw a jug of water, towards which the dying man extended a trembling hand. A truly infernal idea entered his mind. He poured some water into a gourd which hung from his belt, held it to the lips of the wounded man, and then withdrew it.

"Oh! I thirst-that water! ... For pity's sake, give me some!"

"Yes, but on one condition you must tell me your whole history."

"Yes ... but give me water!"

His tormentor allowed him to swallow a mouthful, then overwhelmed him with questions as to his family, his friends and fortune, and compelled him to answer by keeping before his eyes the water which alone could relieve the fever which devoured him. After this often interrupted interrogation, the sufferer sank back exhausted, and almost insensible. But, not yet satisfied, his companion conceived the idea of reviving him with a few drops of brandy, which quickly brought back the fever, and excited his brain sufficiently to enable him to answer fresh questions. The doses of spirit were doubled several times, at the risk of ending the unhappy man's days then and there: Almost delirious, his head feeling as if on fire, his sufferings gave way to a feverish excitement, which took him back to other places and other times: he began to recall the days of his youth and the country where he lived. But his tongue was still fettered by a kind of reserve: his secret thoughts, the private details of his past life were not yet told, and it seemed as though he might die at any moment. Time was passing, night already coming on, and it occurred to the merciless questioner to profit by the gathering darkness. By a few solemn words he aroused the religious feelings of the sufferer, terrified him by speaking of the punishments of another life and the flames of hell, until to the delirious fancy of the sick man he took the form of a judge who could either deliver him to eternal damnation or open the gates of heaven to him. At length, overwhelmed by a voice which resounded in his ear like that of a minister of God, the dying man laid bare his inmost soul before his tormentor, and made his last confession to him.

Yet a few moments, and the executioner—he deserves no other name—hangs over his victim, opens his tunic, seizes some papers and a few coins, half draws his dagger, but thinks better of it; then, contemptuously spurning the victim, as the other surgeon had done—

"I might kill you," he says, "but it would be a useless murder; it would only be hastening your last Sigh by an hour or two, and advancing my claims to your inheritance by the same space of time."

And he adds mockingly:—

"Farewell, my brother!"

The wounded soldier utters a feeble groan; the adventurer leaves the room.

Four months later, a woman sat at the door of a house at one end of the village of Artigues, near Rieux, and played with a child about nine or ten years of age. Still young, she had the brown complexion of Southern women, and her beautiful black hair fell in curls about her face. Her flashing eyes occasionally betrayed hidden passions, concealed, however, beneath an apparent indifference and lassitude, and her wasted form seemed to acknowledge the existence of some secret grief. An observer would have divined a shattered life, a withered happiness, a soul grievously wounded.

Her dress was that of a wealthy peasant; and she wore one of the long gowns with hanging sleeves which were in fashion in the sixteenth century. The house in front of which she sat belonged to her, so also the immense field which adjoined the garden. Her attention was divided between the play of her son and the orders she was giving to an old servant, when an exclamation from the child startled her.

"Mother!" he cried, "mother, there he is!"

She looked where the child pointed, and saw a young boy turning the corner of the street.

"Yes," continued the child, "that is the lad who, when I was playing with the other boys yesterday, called me all sorts of bad names."

"What sort of names, my child?"

"There was one I did not understand, but it must have been a very bad one, for the other boys all pointed at me, and left me alone. He called me—and he said it was only what his mother had told him—he called me a wicked bastard!"

His mother's face became purple with indignation. "What!" she cried, "they dared! ... What an insult!"

"What does this bad word mean, mother?" asked the

child, half frightened by her anger. "Is that what they call poor children who have no father?"

His mother folded him in her arms. "Oh!" she continued, "it is an infamous slander! These people never saw your father, they have only been here six years, and this is the eighth since he went away, but this is abominable! We were married in that church, we came at once to live in this house, which was my marriage portion, and my poor Martin has relations and friends here who will not allow his wife to be insulted—"

"Say rather, his widow," interrupted a solemn voice.

"Ah! uncle!" exclaimed the woman, turning towards an old man who had just emerged from the house.

"Yes, Bertrande," continued the new-comer, "you must get reconciled to the idea that my nephew has ceased to exist. I am sure he was not such a fool as to have remained all this time without letting us hear from him. He was not the fellow to go off at a tangent, on account of a domestic quarrel which you have never vouchsafed to explain to me, and to retain his anger during all these eight years! Where did he go? What did he do? We none of us know, neither you nor I, nor anybody else. He is assuredly dead, and lies in some graveyard far enough from here. May God have mercy on his soul!"

Bertrande, weeping, made the sign of the cross, and bowed her head upon her hands.

"Good-bye, Sanxi," said the uncle, tapping the child's,' cheek. Sanxi turned sulkily away.

There was certainly nothing specially attractive about

the uncle: he belonged to a type which children instinctively dislike, false, crafty, with squinting eyes which continually appeared to contradict his honeyed tongue.

"Bertrande," he said, "your boy is like his father before him, and only answers my kindness with rudeness."

"Forgive him," answered the mother; "he is very young, and does not understand the respect due to his father's uncle. I will teach him better things; he will soon learn that he ought to be grateful for the care you have taken of his little property."

"No doubt, no doubt," said the uncle, trying hard to smile. "I will give you a good account of it, for I shall only have to reckon with you two in future. Come, my dear, believe me, your husband is really dead, and you have sorrowed quite enough for a good-for-nothing fellow. Think no more of him."

So saying, he departed, leaving the poor young woman a prey to the saddest thoughts.

Bertrande de Rolls, naturally gifted with extreme sensibility, on which a careful education had imposed due restraint, had barely completed her twelfth year when she was married to Martin Guerre, a boy of about the same age, such precocious unions being then not uncommon, especially in the Southern provinces. They were generally settled by considerations of family interest, assisted by the extremely early development habitual to the climate. The young couple lived for a long time as brother and sister, and Bertrande, thus early familiar with the idea of domestic happiness, bestowed her whole affection on the youth whom she had been taught to regard as her life's companion. He was the Alpha and Omega of her existence; all her love, all her thoughts, were given to him, and when their marriage was at length completed, the birth of a son seemed only another link in the already long existing bond of union. But, as many wise men have remarked, a uniform happiness, which only attaches women more and more, has often upon men a precisely contrary effect, and so it was with Martin Guerre. Of a lively and excitable temperament, he wearied of a yoke which had been imposed so early, and, anxious to see the world and enjoy some freedom, he one day took advantage of a domestic difference, in which Bertrande owned herself to have been wrong, and left his house and family. He was sought and awaited in vain. Bertrande spent the first month in vainly expecting his return, then she betook herself to prayer; but Heaven appeared deaf to her supplications, the truant returned not. She wished to go in search of him, but the world is wide, and no single trace remained to guide her. What torture for a tender heart! What suffering for a soul thirsting for love! What sleepless nights! What restless vigils! Years passed thus; her son was growing up, yet not a word reached her from the man she loved so much. She spoke often of him to the uncomprehending child, she sought to discover his features in those of her boy, but though she endeavoured to concentrate her whole affection on her son, she realised that there is suffering which maternal love cannot console, and tears which it cannot dry. Consumed by the strength of the sorrow which ever dwelt in her heart, the poor woman was slowly wasting, worn out by the regrets of the past, the vain desires of the present, and the dreary prospect of the future. And now she had been openly insulted, her feelings as a mother wounded to the quirk; and her husband's uncle, instead of defending and consoling her, could give only cold counsel and unsympathetic words!

Pierre Guerre, indeed, was simply a thorough egotist. In his youth he had been charged with usury; no one knew by what means he had become rich, for the little drapery trade which he called his profession did not appear to be very profitable.

After his nephew's departure it seemed only natural that he should pose as the family guardian, and he applied himself to the task of increasing the little income, but without considering himself bound to give any account to Bertrande. So, once persuaded that Martin was no more, he was apparently not unwilling to prolong a situation so much to his own advantage.

Night was fast coming on; in the dim twilight distant objects became confused and indistinct. It was the end of autumn, that melancholy season which suggests so many gloomy thoughts and recalls so many blighted hopes. The child had gone into the house. Bertrande, still sitting at the door, resting her forehead on her hand, thought sadly of her uncle's words; recalling in imagination the past scenes which they suggested, the time of their childhood, when, married so young, they were as yet only playmates, prefacing the graver duties of life by innocent pleasures; then of the love which grew with their increasing age; then of how this love became altered, changing on her side into passion, on his into indifference. She tried to recollect him as he had been on the eve of his departure, young and handsome, carrying his head high, coming home from a fatiguing hunt and sitting by his son's cradle; and then also she remembered bitterly the jealous suspicions she had conceived, the anger with which she had allowed them to escape her, the consequent quarrel, followed by the disappearance of her offended husband, and the eight succeeding years of solitude and mourning. She wept over his desertion; over the desolation of her life, seeing around her only indifferent or selfish people, and caring only to live for her child's sake, who gave her at least a shadowy reflection of the husband she had lost. "Lost—yes, lost for ever!" she said to herself, sighing, and looking again at the fields whence she had so often seen him coming at this same twilight hour, returning to his home for the evening meal. She cast a wandering eye on the distant hills, which showed a black outline against a yet fiery western sky, then let it fall on a little grove of olive trees planted on the farther side of the brook which skirted her dwelling. Everything was calm; approaching night brought silence along with darkness: it was exactly what she saw every evening, but to leave which required always an effort.

    She rose to re-enter the house, when her attention was caught by a movement amongst the trees. For a moment she thought she was mistaken, but the branches again rustled, then parted asunder, and the form of a man appeared on the other side of the brook. Terrified, Bertrande tried to scream, but not a sound escaped her lips; her voice seemed paralyzed by terror, as in an evil dream. And she almost thought it was a dream, for notwithstanding the dark shadows cast around this indistinct semblance, she seemed to recognise features once dear to her. Had her bitter reveries ended by making her the victim of a hallucination? She thought her brain was giving way, and sank on her knees to pray for help. But the figure remained; it stood motionless, with folded arms, silently gazing at her! Then she thought of witchcraft, of evil demons, and superstitious as every one was in those days, she kissed a crucifix which hung from her neck, and fell fainting on the ground. With one spring the phantom crossed the brook and stood beside her.

"Bertrande!" it said in a voice of emotion. She raised her head, uttered a piercing cry, and was clasped in her husband's arms.

The whole village became aware of this event that same evening. The neighbours crowded round Bertrande's door, Martin's friends and relations naturally wishing to see him after this miraculous reappearance, while those who had never known him desired no less to gratify their curiosity; so that the hero of the little drama, instead of remaining quietly at home with his wife, was obliged to exhibit himself publicly in a neighbouring barn. His four sisters burst through the crowd and fell on his neck weeping; his uncle examined him doubtfully at first, then extended his arms. Everybody recognised him, beginning with the old servant Margherite, who had been with the young couple ever since their wedding-day. People observed only that a riper age had strengthened his features, and given more character to his countenance and more development to his powerful figure; also that he had a scar over the right eyebrow, and that he limped slightly. These were the marks of wounds he had received, he said; which now no longer troubled him. He appeared anxious to return to his wife and child, but the crowd insisted on hearing the story of his adventures during his voluntary absence, and he was obliged to satisfy them. Eight years ago, he said, the desire to see more of the world had gained an irresistible mastery over him; he yielded to it, and departed secretly. A natural longing took him to his birthplace in Biscay, where he had seen his surviving relatives. There he met the Cardinal of Burgos, who took him into his service, promising him profit, hard knocks to give and take, and plenty of adventure. Some time after, he left the cardinal's household for that of his brother, who, much against his will, compelled him to follow him to the war and bear arms against the French. Thus he found himself on the Spanish side on the day of St. Quentin, and received a terrible gun-shot wound in the leg. Being carried into a house a an adjoining village, he fell into the hands of a surgeon, who insisted that the leg must be amputated immediately, but who left him for a moment, and never returned. Then he encountered a good old woman, who dressed his wound and nursed him night and day. So that in a few weeks he recovered, and was able to set out for

Artigues, too thankful to return to his house and land, still more to his wife and child, and fully resolved never to leave them again.

Having ended his story, he shook hands with his still wondering neighbours, addressing by name some who had been very young when he left, and who, hearing their names, came forward now as grown men, hardly recognisable, but much pleased at being remembered. He returned his sisters' carresses, begged his uncle's forgiveness for the trouble he had given in his boyhood, recalling with mirth the various corrections received. He mentioned also an Augustinian monk who had taught him to read, and another reverend father, a Capuchin, whose irregular conduct had caused much scandal in the neighbourhood. In short, notwithstanding his prolonged absence, he seemed to have a perfect recollection of places, persons, and things. The good people overwhelmed him with congratulations, vying with one another in praising him for having the good sense to come home, and in describing the grief and the perfect virtue of his Bertrande. Emotion was excited, many wept, and several bottles from Martin Guerre's cellar were emptied. At length the assembly dispersed, uttering many exclamations about the extraordinary chances of Fate, and retired to their own homes, excited, astonished, and gratified, with the one exception of old Pierre Guerre, who had been struck by an unsatisfactory remark made by his nephew, and who dreamed all night about the chances of pecuniary loss augured by the latter's return.

It was midnight before the husband and wife were alone

and able to give vent to their feelings. Bertrande still felt half stupefied; she could not believe her own eyes and ears, nor realise that she saw again in her marriage chamber her husband of eight years ago, him for whom she had wept; whose death she had deplored only a few hours previously. In the sudden shock caused by so much joy succeeding so much grief, she had not been able to express what she felt; her confused ideas were difficult to explain, and she seemed deprived of the powers of speech and reflection. When she became calmer and more capable of analysing her feelings, she was astonished not to feel towards her husband the same affection which had moved her so strongly a few hours before. It was certainly himself, those were the same features, that was the man to whom she had willingly given her hand, her heart, herself, and yet now that she saw him again a cold barrier of shyness, of modesty, seemed to have risen between them. His first kiss, even, had not made her happy: she blushed and felt saddened—a curious result of the long absence! She could not define the changes wrought by years in his appearance: his countenance seemed harsher, yet the lines of his face, his outer man, his whole personality, did not seem altered, but his soul had changed its nature, a different mind looked forth from those eyes. Bertrande knew him for her husband, and yet she hesitated. Even so Penelope, on the, return of Ulysses, required a certain proof to confirm the evidence of her eyes, and her long absent husband had to remind her of secrets known only to herself.

Martin, however, as if he understood Bertrande's feeling

and divined some secret mistrust, used the most tender and affectionate phrases, and even the very pet names which close intimacy had formerly endeared to them.

"My queen," he said, "my beautiful dove, can you not lay aside your resentment? Is it still so strong that no submission can soften it? Cannot my repentance find grace in your eyes? My Bertrande, my Bertha, my Bertranilla, as I used to call you."

She tried to smile, but stopped short, puzzled; the names were the very same, but the inflexion of voice quite different.

Martin took her hands in his. "What pretty hands! Do you still wear my ring? Yes, here it is, and with it the sapphire ring I gave you the day Sanxi was born."

Bertrande did not answer, but she took the child and placed him in his father's arms.

Martin showered caresses on his son, and spoke of the time when he carried him as a baby in the garden, lifting him up to the fruit trees, so that he could reach and try to bite the fruit. He recollected one day when the poor child got his leg terribly torn by thorns, and convinced himself, not without emotion, that the scar could still be seen.

Bertrande was touched by this display of affectionate recollections, and felt vexed at her own coldness. She came up to Martin and laid her hand in his. He said gently—

"My departure caused you great grief: I now repent what I did. But I was young, I was proud, and your reproaches were unjust."

"Ah," said she, "you have not forgotten the cause of our

quarrel?"

"It was little Rose, our neighbour, whom you said I was making love to, because you found us together at the spring in the little wood. I explained that we met only by chance,—besides, she was only a child,—but you would not listen, and in your anger—"

"Ah! forgive me, Martin, forgive me!" she interrupted, in confusion.

"In your blind anger you took up, I know not what, something which lay handy, and flung it at me. And here is the mark," he continued, smiling, "this scar, which is still to be seen."

"Oh, Martin!" Bertrande exclaimed, "can you ever forgive me?"

"As you see," Martin replied, kissing her tenderly.

Much moved, Bertrande swept aside his hair, and looked at the scar visible on his forehead.

"But," she said, with surprise not free from alarm, "this scar seems to me like a fresh one."

"Ah!" Martin explained, with a little embarrassment; "it reopened lately. But I had thought no more about it. Let us forget it, Bertrande; I should not like a recollection which might make you think yourself less dear to me than you once were."

And he drew her upon his knee. She repelled him gently.

"Send the child to bed," said Martin. "Tomorrow shall be for him; to-night you have the first place, Bertrande, you only."

The boy kissed his father and went.

Bertrande came and knelt beside her husband, regarding him attentively with an uneasy smile, which did not appear to please him by any means.

"What is the matter?" said he. "Why do you examine me thus?"

"I do not know—forgive me, oh! forgive me! . . . But the happiness of seeing you was so great and unexpected, it is all like a dream. I must try to become accustomed to it; give me some time to collect myself; let me spend this night in prayer. I ought to offer my joy and my thanksgiving to Almighty God—"

"Not so," interrupted her husband, passing his arms round her neck and stroking her beautiful hair. "No; 'tis to me that your first thoughts are due. After so much weariness, my rest is in again beholding you, and my happiness after so many trials will be found in your love. That hope has supported me throughout, and I long to be assured that it is no illusion." So saying, he endeavoured to raise her.

"Oh," she murmured, "I pray you leave me."

"What!" he exclaimed angrily. "Bertrande, is this your love? Is it thus you keep faith with me? You will make me doubt the evidence of your friends; you will make me think that indifference, or even another love——"

"You insult me," said Bertrande, rising to her feet.

He caught her in his arms. "No, no; I think nothing which could wound you, my queen, and I believe your fidelity, even as before, you know, on that first journey, when you wrote me these loving letters which I have treasured ever since. Here they are." And he drew forth some papers, on which Bertrande recognised her own handwriting. "Yes," he continued, "I have read and—re-read them.... See, you spoke then of your love and the sorrows of absence. But why all this trouble and terror? You tremble, just as you did when I first received you from your father's hands.... It was here, in this very room.... You begged me then to leave you, to let you spend the night in prayer; but I insisted, do you remember? and pressed you to my heart, as I do now."

"Oh," she murmured weakly, "have pity!"

But the words were intercepted by a kiss, and the remembrance of the past, the happiness of the present, resumed their sway; the imaginary terrors were forgotten, and the curtains closed around the marriage-bed.

The next day was a festival in the village of Artigues. Martin returned the visits of all who had come to welcome him the previous night, and there were endless recognitions and embracings. The young men remembered that he had played with them when they were little; the old men, that they had been at his wedding when he was only twelve.

The women remembered having envied Bertrande, especially the pretty Rose, daughter of Marcel, the apothecary, she who had roused the demon of jealousy in, the poor wife's heart. And Rose knew quite well that the jealousy was not without some cause; for Martin had indeed shown her attention, and she was unable to see him again without emotion. She was now the wife of a rich peasant, ugly, old, and jealous, and she compared, sighing, her unhappy lot with that of her more fortunate neighbour. Martin's sisters detained him amongst them, and spoke of their childish games and of their parents, both dead in Biscay. Martin dried the tears which flowed at these recollections of the past, and turned their thoughts to rejoicing. Banquets were given and received. Martin invited all his relations and former friends; an easy gaiety prevailed. It was remarked that the hero of the feast refrained from wine; he was thereupon reproached, but answered that on account of the wounds he had received he was obliged to avoid excess. The excuse was admitted, the result of Martin's precautions being that he kept a clear head on his shoulders, while all the rest had their tongues loosed by drunkenness.

"Ah!" exclaimed one of the guests, who had studied a little medicine, "Martin is quite right to be afraid of drink. Wounds which have thoroughly healed may be reopened and inflamed by intemperance, and wine in the case of recent wounds is deadly poison. Men have died on the field of battle in an hour or two merely because they had swallowed a little brandy."

Martin Guerre grew pale, and began a conversation with the pretty Rose, his neighbour. Bertrande observed this, but without uneasiness; she had suffered too much from her former suspicions, besides her husband showed her so much affection that she was now quite happy.

When the first few days were over, Martin began to look into his affairs. His property had suffered by his long absence, and he was obliged to go to Biscay to claim his little estate there, the law having already laid hands upon it. It was several months before, by dint of making judicious sacrifices, he could regain possession of the house and fields which had belonged to his father. This at last accomplished, he returned to Artigues, in order to resume the management of his wife's property, and with this end in view, about eleven months after his return, he paid a visit to his uncle Pierre.

Pierre was expecting him; he was extremely polite, desired Martin, to sit down, overwhelmed him with compliments, knitting his brows as he discovered that his nephew decidedly meant business. Martin broke silence.

"Uncle," he said, "I come to thank you for the care you have taken of my wife's property; she could never have managed it alone. You have received the income in the family interest: as a good guardian, I expected no less from your affection. But now that I have returned, and am free from other cares, we will go over the accounts, if you please."

His uncle coughed and cleared his voice before replying, then said slowly, as if counting his words—

"It is all accounted for, my dear nephew; Heaven be praised! I don't owe you anything."

"What!" exclaimed the astonished Martin, "but the whole income?"

"Was well and properly employed in the maintenance of your wife and child."

"What! a thousand livres for that? And Bertrande lived alone, so quietly and simply! Nonsense! it is impossible."

"Any surplus," resumed the old man, quite unmoved,—"any surplus went to pay the expenses of seed-time and harvest."

"What! at a time when labour costs next to nothing?"

"Here is the account," said Pierre.

"Then the account is a false one," returned his nephew.

Pierre thought it advisable to appear extremely offended and angry, and Martin, exasperated at his evident dishonesty, took still higher ground, and threatened to bring an action against him. Pierre ordered him to leave the house, and suiting actions to words, took hold of his arm to enforce his departure. Martin, furious, turned and raised his fist to strike.

"What! strike your uncle, wretched boy!" exclaimed the old man.

Martin's hand dropped, but he left the house uttering reproaches and insults, among which Pierre distinguished—

"Cheat that you are!"

"That is a word I shall remember," cried the angry old man, slamming his door violently.

Martin brought an action before the judge at Rieux, and in course of time obtained a decree, which, reviewing the accounts presented by Pierre, disallowed them, and condemned the dishonest guardian to pay his nephew four hundred livres for each year of his administration. The day on which this sum had to be disbursed from his strong box the old usurer vowed vengeance, but until he could gratify his hatred he was forced to conceal it, and to receive attempts at reconciliation with a friendly smile. It was not until six months later, on the occasion of a joyous festivity, that Martin again set foot in his uncle's house. The bells were ringing for the birth of a child, there was great gaiety at Bertrande's house, where all the guests were waiting on the threshold for the godfather in order to take the infant to church, and when Martin appeared, escorting his uncle, who was adorned with a huge bouquet for the occasion, and who now came forward and took the hand of Rose, the pretty godmother, there were cries of joy on all sides. Bertrande was delighted at this reconciliation, and dreamed only of happiness. She was so happy now, her long sorrow was atoned for, her regret was at an end, her prayers seemed to have been heard, the long interval between the former delights and the present seemed wiped out as if the bond of union had never been broken, and if she remembered her grief at all, it was only to intensify the new joys by comparison. She loved her husband more than ever; he was full of affection for her, and she was grateful for his love. The past had now no shadow, the future no cloud, and the birth of a daughter, drawing still closer the links which united them, seemed a new pledge of felicity. Alas! the horizon which appeared so bright and clear to the poor woman was doomed soon again to be overcast.

    The very evening of the christening party, a band of musicians and jugglers happened to pass through the village, and the inhabitants showed themselves liberal. Pierre asked questions, and found that the leader of the band was a Spaniard. He invited the man to his own house, and remained closeted with him for nearly an hour, dismissing him at length with a refilled purse. Two days later the old man announced to the family that he was going to Picardy to see a former partner on a matter of business, and he departed accordingly, saying he should return before long.

The day on which Bertrande again saw her uncle was, indeed, a terrible one. She was sitting by the cradle of the lately-born infant, watching for its awakening, when the door opened, and Pierre Guerre strode in. Bertrande drew back with an instinct of terror as soon as she saw him, for his expression was at once wicked and joyful—an expression of gratified hate, of mingled rage and triumph, and his smile was terrible to behold. She did not venture to speak, but motioned him to a seat. He came straight up to her, and raising his head, said loudly—

"Kneel down at once, madame—kneel down, and ask pardon from Almighty God!"

"Are you mad, Pierre?" she replied, gazing at him in astonishment.

"You, at least, ought to know that I am not."

"Pray for forgiveness—I—! and what for, in Heaven's name?"

"For the crime in which you are an accomplice."

"Please explain yourself."

"Oh!" said Pierre, with bitter irony, "a woman always thinks herself innocent as long as her sin is hidden; she thinks the truth will never be known, and her conscience goes quietly to sleep, forgetting her faults. Here is a woman who thought her sins nicely concealed; chance favoured her: an absent husband, probably no more; another man so exactly like him in height, face, and manner that everyone else is deceived! Is it strange that a weak, sensitive woman, wearied of widowhood, should willingly allow herself to be imposed on?"

Bertrande listened without understanding; she tried to interrupt, but Pierre went on—

"It was easy to accept this stranger without having to blush for it, easy to give him the name and the rights of a husband! She could even appear faithful while really guilty; she could seem constant, though really fickle; and she could, under a veil of mystery, at once reconcile her honour, her duty—perhaps even her love."

"What on earth do you mean?" cried Bertrande, wringing her hands in terror.

"That you are countenancing an impostor who is not your husband."

Feeling as if the ground were passing from beneath her, Bertrande staggered, and caught at the nearest piece of furniture to save herself from falling; then, collecting all her strength to meet this extraordinary attack, she faced the old man.

"What! my husband, your nephew, an impostor!"

"Don't you know it?" "I!!"

This cry, which came from her heart, convinced Pierre that she did not know, and that she had sustained a terrible shock. He continued more quietly—

"What, Bertrande, is it possible you were really deceived?"

"Pierre, you are killing me; your words are torture. No more mystery, I entreat. What do you know? What do you suspect? Tell me plainly at once."

"Have you courage to hear it?"

"I must," said the trembling woman.

"God is my witness that I would willingly have kept it from you, but you must know; if only for the safety of your soul entangled in so deadly a snare,... there is yet time, if you follow my advice. Listen: the man with whom you are living, who dares to call himself Martin Guerre, is a cheat, an impostor——"

"How dare you say so?"

"Because I have discovered it. Yes, I had always a vague suspicion, an uneasy feeling, and in spite of the marvellous resemblance I could never feel as if he were really my sister's child. The day he raised his hand to strike me—yes, that day I condemned him utterly.... Chance has justified me! A wandering Spaniard, an old soldier, who spent a night in the village here, was also present at the battle of St. Quentin, and saw Martin Guerre receive a terrible gunshot wound in the leg. After the battle, being wounded, he betook himself to the neighbouring village, and distinctly heard a surgeon in the next room say that a wounded man must have his leg amputated, and would very likely not survive the operation. The door opened, he saw the sufferer, and knew him for Martin Guerre. So much the Spaniard told me. Acting on this information, I went on pretence of business to the village he named, I questioned the inhabitants, and this is what I learned."

"Well?" said Bertrande, pale, and gasping with emotion.

"I learned that the wounded man had his leg taken off, and, as the surgeon predicted, he must have died in a few hours, for he was never seen again."

Bertrande remained a few moments as if annihilated by this appalling revelation; then, endeavoring to repel the horrible thought—

"No," she cried, "no, it is impossible! It is a lie intended to ruin him-to ruin us all."

"What! you do not believe me?"

"No, never, never!"

"Say rather you pretend to disbelieve me: the truth has pierced your heart, but you wish to deny it. Think, however, of the danger to your immortal soul."

"Silence, wretched man!... No, God would not send me so terrible a trial. What proof can you show of the truth of your words?"

"The witnesses I have mentioned."

"Nothing more?"

"No, not as yet."

"Fine proofs indeed! The story of a vagabond who flattered your hatred in hope of a reward, the gossip of a distant village, the recollections of ten years back, and finally, your own word, the word of a man who seeks only revenge, the word of a man who swore to make Martin pay dearly for the results of his own avarice, a man of furious passions such as yours! No, Pierre, no, I do not believe you, and I never will!"

"Other people may perhaps be less incredulous, and if I accuse him publicly——"

"Then I shall contradict you publicly!" And coming quickly forward, her eyes shining with virtuous anger—

"Leave this house, go," she said; "it is you yourself who are the impostor—go!"

"I shall yet know how to convince everyone, and will make you acknowledge it," cried the furious old man.

He went out, and Bertrande sank exhausted into a chair. All the strength which had supported her against Pierre vanished as soon as she was alone, and in spite of her resistance to suspicion, the terrible light of doubt penetrated her heart, and extinguished the pure torch of trustfulness which had guided her hitherto—a doubt, alas! which attacked at once her honour and her love, for she loved with all a woman's tender affection. Just as actual poison gradually penetrates and circulates through the whole system, corrupting the blood and affecting the very sources of life until it causes the destruction of the whole body, so does that mental poison, suspicion, extend its ravages in the soul which has received it. Bertrande remembered with terror her first feelings at the sight of the returned Martin Guerre, her involuntary repugnance, her astonishment at not feeling more in touch with the husband whom she had so sincerely regretted. She remembered also, as if she saw it for the first time, that Martin, formerly quick, lively, and hasty tempered, now seemed thoughtful, and fully master of himself.

This change of character she had supposed due to the natural development of age, she now trembled at the idea of another possible cause. Some other little details began to occur to her mind—the forgetfulness or abstraction of her husband as to a few insignificant things; thus it sometimes happened that he did not answer to his name of Martin, also that he mistook the road to a hermitage, formerly well known to them both, and again that he could not answer when addressed in Basque, although he him self had taught her the little she knew of this language. Besides, since his return, he would never write in her presence, did he fear that she would notice some difference? She had paid little or no attention to these trifles; now, pieced together, they assumed an alarming importance. An appalling terror seized Bertrande: was she to remain in this uncertainty, or should she seek an explanation which might prove her destruction? And how discover the truth—by questioning the guilty man, by noting his confusion, his change of colour, by forcing a confession from him? But she had lived with him for two years, he was the father of her child, she could not ruin him without ruining herself, and, an explanation once sought, she could neither punish him and escape disgrace, nor pardon him without sharing his guilt. To reproach him with his conduct and then keep silence would destroy her peace for ever; to cause a scandal by denouncing him would bring dishonour upon herself and her child. Night found her involved in these hideous perplexities, too weak to surmount them; an icy chill came over her, she went to bed, and awoke in a high fever. For several days she hovered between life and death, and Martin Guerre bestowed the most tender care upon her. She was greatly moved thereby, having one of those impressionable minds which recognise kindness fully as much as injury. When she was a little recovered and her mental power began to return, she had only a vague recollection of what had occurred, and thought she had had a frightful dream. She asked if Pierre Guerre had been to see her, and found he had not been near the house. This could only be explained by the scene which had taken place, and she then recollected all the accusation Pierre had made, her own observations which had confirmed it, all her grief and trouble. She inquired about the village news. Pierre, evidently, had kept silence why? Had he seen that his suspicions were unjust, or was he only seeking further evidence? She sank back into her cruel uncertainty, and resolved to watch Martin closely, before deciding as to his guilt or innocence.

How was she to suppose that God had created two faces so exactly alike, two beings precisely similar, and then sent them together into the world, and on the same track, merely to compass the ruin of an unhappy woman! A terrible idea took possession of her mind, an idea not uncommon in an age of superstition, namely, that the Enemy himself could assume human form, and could borrow the semblance of a dead man in order to capture another soul for his infernal kingdom. Acting on this idea, she hastened to the church, paid for masses to be said, and prayed fervently. She expected every day to see the demon forsake the body he had animated, but her vows, offerings, and prayers had no result. But Heaven sent her an idea which she wondered had not occurred to her sooner. "If the Tempter," she said to herself, "has taken the form of my beloved husband, his power being supreme for evil, the resemblance would be exact, and no difference, however slight, would exist. If, however, it is only another man who resembles him, God must have made them with some slight distinguishing marks."

She then remembered, what she had not thought of before, having been quite unsuspicious before her uncle's accusation, and nearly out of her mind between mental and bodily suffering since. She remembered that on her husband's left shoulder, almost on the neck, there used to be one of those small, almost imperceptible, but ineffaceable birthmarks. Martin wore his hair very long, it was difficult to see if the mark were there or not. One night, while he slept, Bertrande cut away a lock of hair from the place where this sign ought to be—it was not there!

Convinced at length of the deception, Bertrande suffered inexpressible anguish. This man whom she had loved and respected for two whole years, whom she had taken to her heart as a husband bitterly mourned for—this man was a cheat, an infamous impostor, and she, all unknowing, was yet a guilty woman! Her child was illegitimate, and the curse of Heaven was due to this sacrilegious union. To complete the misfortune, she was already expecting another infant. She would have killed herself, but her religion and the love of her children forbade it. Kneeling before her child's cradle, she entreated pardon from the father of the one for the father of the other. She would not bring herself to proclaim aloud their infamy.

"Oh!" she said, "thou whom I loved, thou who art no more, thou knowest no guilty thought ever entered my mind! When I saw this man, I thought I beheld thee; when I was happy, I thought I owed it to thee; it was thee whom I loved in him. Surely thou dost not desire that by a public avowal I should bring shame and disgrace on these children and on myself."

She rose calm and strengthened: it seemed as if a heavenly inspiration had marked out her duty. To suffer in silence, such was the course she adopted,—a life of sacrifice and self-denial which she offered to God as an expiation for her involuntary sin. But who can understand the workings of the human heart? This man whom she ought to have loathed, this man who had made her an innocent partner in his crime, this unmasked impostor whom she should have beheld only with disgust, she-loved him! The force of habit, the ascendancy he had obtained over her, the love he had shown her, a thousand sympathies felt in her inmost heart, all these had so much influence, that, instead of accusing and cursing him, she sought to excuse him on the plea of a passion to which, doubtless, he had yielded when usurping the name and place of another. She feared punishment for him yet more than disgrace for herself, and though resolved to no longer allow him the rights purchased by crime, she yet trembled at the idea of losing his love. It was this above all which decided her to keep eternal silence about her discovery; one single word which proved that his imposture was known would raise an insurmountable barrier between them.

To conceal her trouble entirely was, however, beyond her power; her eyes frequently showed traces of her secret tears. Martin several times asked the cause of her sorrow; she tried to smile and excuse herself, only immediately sinking back into her gloomy thoughts. Martin thought it mere caprice; he observed her loss of colour, her hollow cheeks, and concluded that age was impairing her beauty, and became less attentive to her. His absences became longer and more frequent, and he did not conceal his impatience and annoyance at being watched; for her looks hung upon his, and she observed his coldness and change with much grief. Having sacrificed all in order to retain his love, she now saw it slowly slipping away from her.

Another person also observed attentively. Pierre Guerre since his explanation with Bertrande had apparently discovered no more evidence, and did not dare to bring an accusation without some positive proofs. Consequently he lost no chance of watching the proceedings of his supposed nephew, silently hoping that chance might put him on the track of a discovery. He also concluded from Bertrande's state of melancholy that she had convinced herself of the fraud, but had resolved to conceal it.

Martin was then endeavoring to sell a part of his property, and this necessitated frequent interviews with the lawyers of the neighbouring town. Twice in the week he went to Rieux, and to make the journey easier, used to start horseback about seven in the evening, sleep at Rieux, and return the following afternoon. This arrangement did not escape his enemy's notice, who was not long in convincing himself that part of the time ostensibly spent on this journey was otherwise employed.

Towards ten o'clock on the evening of a dark night, the door of a small house lying about half a gunshot from the village opened gently for the exit of a man wrapped in a large cloak, followed by a young woman, who accompanied him some distance. Arrived at the parting point, they separated with a tender kiss and a few murmured words of adieu; the lover took his horse, which was fastened to a tree, mounted, and rode off towards Rieux. When the sounds died away, the woman turned slowly and sadly towards her home, but as she approached the door a man suddenly turned the corner of the house and barred her away. Terrified, she was on the point of crying for help, when he seized her arm and ordered her to be silent.

"Rose," he whispered, "I know everything: that man is your lover. In order to receive him safely, you send your old husband to sleep by means of a drug stolen from your father's shop. This intrigue has been going on for a month; twice a week, at seven o'clock, your door is opened to this man, who does not proceed on his way to the town until ten. I know your lover: he is my nephew."

Petrified with terror, Rose fell on her knees and implored mercy.

"Yes," replied Pierre, "you may well be frightened: I have your secret. I have only to publish it and you are ruined for ever:"

You will not do it! "entreated the guilty woman, clasping her hands.

"I have only to tell your husband," continued Pierre, "that his wife has dishonoured him, and to explain the reason of his unnaturally heavy sleep."

"He will kill me!"

"No doubt: he is jealous, he is an Italian, he will know how to avenge himself—even as I do."

"But I never did you any harm," Rose cried in despair. "Oh! have pity, have mercy, and spare me!"

"On one condition."

"What is it?"

"Come with me."

Terrified almost out of her mind, Rose allowed him to lead her away.

Bertrande had just finished her evening prayer, and was preparing for bed, when she was startled by several knocks at her door. Thinking that perhaps some neighbour was in need of help, she opened it immediately, and to her astonishment beheld a dishevelled woman whom Pierre grasped by the arm. He exclaimed vehemently—

"Here is thy judge! Now, confess all to Bertrande!"

Bertrande did not at once recognise the woman, who fell at her feet, overcome by Pierre's threats.

"Tell the truth here," he continued, "or I go and tell it to your husband, at your own home!"—"Ah! madame, kill me," said the unhappy creature, hiding her face; "let me rather die by your hand than his!"

Bertrande, bewildered, did not understand the position in the least, but she recognised Rose—

"But what is the matter, madame? Why are you here at this hour, pale and weeping? Why has my uncle dragged you hither? I am to judge you, does he say? Of what crime are you guilty?"

"Martin might answer that, if he were here," remarked Pierre.

A lightning flash of jealousy shot through Bertrande's soul at these words, all her former suspicions revived.

"What!" she said, "my husband! What do you mean?"

"That he left this woman's house only a little while ago, that for a month they have been meeting secretly. You are betrayed: I have seen them and she does not dare to deny it."

"Have mercy!" cried Rose, still kneeling.

The cry was a confession. Bertrande became pate as death. "O God!" she murmured, "deceived, betrayed—and by him!"

"For a month past," repeated the old man.

"Oh! the wretch," she continued, with increasing passion; "then his whole life is a lie! He has abused my credulity, he now abuses my love! He does not know me! He thinks he can trample on me—me, in whose power are his fortune, his honour, his very life itself!"

Then, turning to Rose—

"And you, miserable woman! by what unworthy artifice

did you gain his love? Was it by witchcraft? or some poisonous philtre learned from your worthy father?"

"Alas! no, madame; my weakness is my only crime, and also my only excuse. I loved him, long ago, when I was only a young girl, and these memories have been my ruin."

"Memories? What! did you also think you were loving the same man? Are you also his dupe? Or are you only pretending, in order to find a rag of excuse to cover your wickedness?"

It was now Rose who failed to understand; Bertrande continued, with growing excitement—

"Yes, it was not enough to usurp the rights of a husband and father, he thought to play his part still better by deceiving the mistress also . . . . Ah! it is amusing, is it not? You also, Rose, you thought he was your old lover! Well, I at least am excusable, I the wife, who only thought she was faithful to her husband!"

"What does it all mean?" asked the terrified Rose.

"It means that this man is an impostor and that I will unmask him. Revenge! revenge!"

Pierre came forward. "Bertrande," he said, "so long as I thought you were happy, when I feared to disturb your peace, I was silent, I repressed my just indignation, and I spared the usurper of the name and rights of my nephew. Do you now give me leave to speak?"

"Yes," she replied in a hollow voice.

"You will not contradict me?"

By way of answer she sat down by the table and wrote

a few hasty lines with a trembling hand, then gave them to Pierre, whose eyes sparkled with joy.

"Yes," he said, "vengeance for him, but for her pity. Let this humiliation be her only punishment. I promised silence in return for confession, will you grant it?"

Bertrande assented with a contemptuous gesture.

"Go, fear not," said the old man, and Rose went out. Pierre also left the house.

Left to herself, Bertrande felt utterly worn out by so much emotion; indignation gave way to depression. She began to realise what she had done, and the scandal which would fall on her own head. Just then her baby awoke, and held out its arms, smiling, and calling for its father. Its father, was he not a criminal? Yes! but was it for her to ruin him, to invoke the law, to send him to death, after having taken him to her heart, to deliver him to infamy which would recoil on her own head and her child's and on the infant which was yet unborn? If he had sinned before God, was it not for God to punish him? If against herself, ought she not rather to overwhelm him with contempt? But to invoke the help, of strangers to expiate this offence; to lay bare the troubles of her life, to unveil the sanctuary of the nuptial couch—in short, to summon the whole world to behold this fatal scandal, was not that what in her imprudent anger she had really done? She repented bitterly of her haste, she sought to avert the consequences, and notwithstanding the night and the bad weather, she hurried at once to Pierre's dwelling, hoping at all costs to withdraw her denunciation. He was not there: he had at once taken a horse and started for Rieux. Her accusation was already on its way to the magistrates!

At break of day the house where Martin Guerre lodged when at Rieux was surrounded by soldiers. He came forward with confidence and inquired what was wanted. On hearing the accusation, he changed colour slightly, then collected himself, and made no resistance. When he came before the judge, Bertrande's petition was read to him, declaring him to be "an impostor, who falsely, audaciously, and treacherously had deceived her by taking the name and assuming the person of Martin Guerre," and demanding that he should be required to entreat pardon from God, the king, and herself.

The prisoner listened calmly to the charge, and met it courageously, only evincing profound surprise at such a step being taken by a wife who had lived with him for two years since his return, and who only now thought of disputing the rights he had so long enjoyed. As he was ignorant both of Bertrande's suspicions and their confirmation, and also of the jealousy which had inspired her accusation, his astonishment was perfectly natural, and did not at all appear to be assumed. He attributed the whole charge to the machinations of his uncle, Pierre Guerre; an old man, he said, who, being governed entirely by avarice and the desire of revenge, now disputed his name and rights, in order the better to deprive him of his property, which might be worth from sixteen to eighteen hundred livres. In order to attain his end, this wicked man had not hesitated to pervert his wife's mind, and at the risk of her own dishonour had instigated this calumnious charge—a horrible and unheard-of thing in the mouth of a lawful wife. "Ah! I do not blame her," he cried; "she must suffer more than I do, if she really entertains doubts such as these; but I deplore her readiness to listen to these extraordinary calumnies originated by my enemy."

The judge was a good deal impressed by so much assurance. The accused was relegated to prison, whence he was brought two days later to encounter a formal examination.

He began by explaining the cause of his long absence, originating, he said, in a domestic quarrel, as his wife well remembered. He there related his life during these eight years. At first he wandered over the country, wherever his curiosity and the love of travel led him. He then had crossed the frontier, revisited Biscay, where he was born, and having entered the service of the Cardinal of Burgos, he passed thence into the army of the King of Spain. He was wounded at the battle of St. Quentin, conveyed to a neighbouring village, where he recovered, although threatened with amputation. Anxious to again behold his wife and child, his other relations and the land of his adoption, he returned to Artigues, where he was immediately recognised by everyone, including the identical Pierre Guerre, his uncle, who now had the cruelty to disavow him. In fact, the latter had shown him special affection up to the day when Martin required an account of his stewardship. Had he only had the cowardice to sacrifice his money and thereby defraud his children, he would not to-day be charged as an impostor. "But," continued Martin, "I resisted, and a violent quarrel ensued, in which anger perhaps carried me too far; Pierre Guerre, cunning and revengeful, has waited in silence. He has taken his time and his measures to organise this plot, hoping thereby to obtain his ends, to bring justice to the help of his avarice, and to acquire the spoils he coveted, and revenge for his defeat, by means of a sentence obtained from the scruples of the judges." Besides these explanations, which did not appear wanting in probability, Martin vehemently protested his innocence, demanding that his wife should be confronted with him, and declaring that in his presence she would not sustain the charge of personation brought against him, and that her mind not being animated by the blind hatred which dominated his persecutor, the truth would undoubtedly prevail.

He now, in his turn, demanded that the judge should acknowledge his innocence, and prove it by condemning his calumniators to the punishment invoked against himself; that his wife, Bertrande de Rolls, should be secluded in some house where her mind could no longer be perverted, and, finally, that his innocence should be declared, and expenses and compensations awarded him.

After this speech, delivered with warmth, and with every token of sincerity, he answered without difficulty all the interrogations of the judge. The following are some of the questions and answers, just as they have come down to us:—

"In what part of Biscay were you born?"

"In the village of Aymes, province of Guipuscoa."

"What were the names of your parents?"

"Antonio Guerre and Marie Toreada."

"Are they still living?"

"My father died June 15th, 1530; my mother survived him three years and twelve days."

"Have you any brothers and sisters?"

"I had one brother, who only lived three months. My four sisters, Inez, Dorothea, Marietta, and Pedrina, all came to live at Artigues when I did; they are there still, and they all recognised me."

"What is the date of your marriage?"

"January 10, 1539."

"Who were present at the ceremony?"

"My father-in-law, my mother-in-law, my uncle, my two sisters, Maitre Marcel and his daughter Rose; a neighbour called Claude Perrin, who got drunk at the wedding feast; also Giraud, the poet, who composed verses in our honour."

"Who was the priest who married you?"

"The old cure, Pascal Guerin, whom I did not find alive when I returned."

"What special circumstances occurred on the wedding-day?"

"At midnight exactly, our neighbour, Catherine Boere, brought us the repast which is known as 'medianoche.' This woman has recognised me, as also our old Marguerite, who has remained with us ever since the wedding."

"What is the date of your son's birth?"

"February 10, 1548, nine years after our marriage. I was only twelve when the ceremony took place, and did not arrive at manhood till several years later."

"Give the date of your leaving Artigues."

"It was in August 1549. As I left the village, I met Claude Perrin and the cure Pascal, and took leave of them. I went towards Beauvais, end I passed through Orleans, Bourges, Limoges, Bordeaux, and Toulouse. If you want the names of people whom I saw and to whom I spoke, you can have them. What more can I say?"

Never, indeed, was there a more apparently veracious statement! All the doings of Martin Guerre seemed to be most faithfully described, and surely only himself could thus narrate his own actions. As the historian remarks, alluding to the story of Amphitryon, Mercury himself could not better reproduce all Sosia's actions, gestures, and words, than did the false Martin Guerre those of the real one.

In accordance with the demand of the accused, Bertrande de Rolls was detained in seclusion, in order to remove her from the influence of Pierre Guerre. The latter, however, did not waste time, and during the month spent in examining the witnesses cited by Martin, his diligent enemy, guided by some vague traces, departed on a journey, from which he did not return alone.

All the witnesses bore out the statement of the accused; the latter heard this in prison, and rejoiced, hoping for a speedy release. Before long he was again brought before the judge, who told him that his deposition had been confirmed by all the witnesses examined.

"Do you know of no others?" continued the magistrate.

"Have you no relatives except those you have mentioned?"

"I have no others," answered the prisoner.

"Then what do you say to this man?" said the judge, opening a door.

An old man issued forth, who fell on the prisoner's neck, exclaiming, "My nephew!"

Martin trembled in every limb, but only for a moment. Promptly recovering himself, and gazing calmly at the newcomer, he asked coolly—

"And who may you be?"

"What!" said the old man, "do you not know me? Dare you deny me?—me, your mother's brother, Carbon Barreau, the old soldier! Me, who dandled you on my knee in your infancy; me, who taught you later to carry a musket; me, who met you during the war at an inn in Picardy, when you fled secretly. Since then I have sought you everywhere; I have spoken of you, and described your face and person, until a worthy inhabitant of this country offered to bring me hither, where indeed I did not expect to find my sister's son imprisoned and fettered as a malefactor. What is his crime, may it please your honour?"

"You shall hear," replied the magistrate. "Then you identify the prisoner as your nephew? You affirm his name to be—-?"

"Arnauld du Thill, also called 'Pansette,' after his father, Jacques Pansa. His mother was Therese Barreau, my sister, and he was born in the village of Sagias."

"What have you to say?" demanded the judge, turning to

the accused.

"Three things," replied the latter, unabashed, "this man is either mad, or he has been suborned to tell lies, or he is simply mistaken."

The old man was struck dumb with astonishment. But his supposed nephew's start of terror had not been lost upon the judge, also much impressed by the straightforward frankness of Carbon Barreau. He caused fresh investigations to be made, and other inhabitants of Sagias were summoned to Rieux, who one and all agreed in identifying the accused as the same Arnauld du Thill who had been born and had grown up under their very eyes. Several deposed that as he grew up he had taken to evil courses, and become an adept in theft and lying, not fearing even to take the sacred name of God in vain, in order to cover the untruth of his daring assertions. From such testimony the judge naturally concluded that Arnauld du Thill was quite capable of carrying on, an imposture, and that the impudence which he displayed was natural to his character. Moreover, he noted that the prisoner, who averred that he was born in Biscay, knew only a few words of the Basque language, and used these quite wrongly. He heard later another witness who deposed that the original Martin Guerre was a good wrestler and skilled in the art of fence, whereas the prisoner, having wished to try what he could do, showed no skill whatever. Finally, a shoemaker was interrogated, and his evidence was not the least damning. Martin Guerre, he declared, required twelve holes to lace his boots, and his surprise had been great when he found those of the prisoner had only nine. Considering all these points, and the cumulative evidence, the judge of Rieux set aside the favourable testimony, which he concluded had been the outcome of general credulity, imposed on by an extraordinary resemblance. He gave due weight also to Bertrande's accusation, although she had never confirmed it, and now maintained an obstinate silence; and he pronounced a judgment by which Arnauld du Thill was declared "attainted and convicted of imposture, and was therefore condemned to be beheaded; after which his body should be divided into four quarters, and exposed at the four corners of the town."

This sentence, as soon as it was known, caused much diversity of opinion in the town. The prisoner's enemies praised the wisdom of the judge, and those less prejudiced condemned his decision; as such conflicting testimony left room for doubt. Besides, it was thought that the possession of property and the future of the children required much consideration, also that the most absolute certainty was demanded before annulling a past of two whole years, untroubled by any counter claim whatever.

The condemned man appealed from this sentence to the Parliament of Toulouse. This court decided that the case required more careful consideration than had yet been given to it, and began by ordering Arnauld du Thill to be confronted with Pierre Guerre and Bertrande de Rolls.

Who can say what feelings animate a man who, already once condemned, finds himself subjected to a second trial?

The torture scarcely ended begins again, and Hope, though reduced to a shadow, regains her sway over his imagination, which clings to her skirts, as it were, with desperation. The exhausting efforts must be recommenced; it is the last struggle—a struggle which is more desperate in proportion as there is less strength to maintain it. In this case the defendant was not one of those who are easily cast down; he collected all his energy, all his courage, hoping to come victoriously out of the new combat which lay before him.

The magistrates assembled in the great hall of the Parliament, and the prisoner appeared before them. He had first to deal with Pierre, and confronted him calmly, letting him speak, without showing any emotion. He then replied with indignant reproaches, dwelling on Pierre's greed and avarice, his vows of vengeance, the means employed to work upon Bertrande, his secret manoeuvres in order to gain his ends, and the unheard-of animosity displayed in hunting up accusers, witnesses, and calumniators. He defied Pierre to prove that he was not Martin Guerre, his nephew, inasmuch as Pierre had publicly acknowledged and embraced him, and his tardy suspicions only dated from the time of their violent quarrel. His language was so strong and vehement, that Pierre became confused and was unable to answer, and the encounter turned entirely in Arnauld's favour, who seemed to overawe his adversary from a height of injured innocence, while the latter appeared as a disconcerted slanderer.

The scene of his confrontation with Bertrande took a wholly different character. The poor woman, pale, cast down, worn by sorrow, came staggering before the tribunal, in an almost fainting condition. She endeavoured to collect herself, but as soon as she saw the prisoner she hung her head and covered her face with her hands. He approached her and besought her in the gentlest accents not to persist in an accusation which might send him to the scaffold, not thus to avenge any sins he might have committed against her, although he could not reproach himself with any really serious fault.

Bertrande started, and murmured in a whisper, "And Rose?"

"Ah!" Arnauld exclaimed, astonished at this revelation.

His part was instantly taken. Turning to the judges—

"Gentlemen," he said, "my wife is a jealous woman! Ten years ago, when I left her, she had formed these suspicions; they were the cause of my voluntary exile. To-day she again accuses me of, guilty relations with the same person; I neither deny nor acknowledge them, but I affirm that it is the blind passion of jealousy which, aided by my uncle's suggestions, guided my wife's hand when she signed this denunciation."

Bertrande remained silent.

"Do you dare," he continued, turning towards her,—"do you dare to swear before God that jealousy did not inspire you with the wish to ruin me?"

"And you," she replied, "dare you swear that I was deceived in my suspicions?"

"You see, gentlemen," exclaimed the prisoner triumphantly, "her jealousy breaks forth before your eyes. Whether I am, or am not, guilty of the sin she attributes to me, is not the question for you to decide. Can you conscientiously admit the testimony of a woman who, after publicly acknowledging me, after receiving me in her house, after living two years in perfect amity with me, has, in a fit of angry vengeance, thought she could give the lie to all her wards and actions? Ah! Bertrande," he continued, "if it only concerned my life I think I could forgive a madness of which your love is both the cause and the excuse, but you are a mother, think of that! My punishment will recoil on the head of my daughter, who is unhappy enough to have been born since our reunion, and also on our unborn child, which you condemn beforehand to curse the union which gave it being. Think of this, Bertrande, you will have to answer before God for what you are now doing!"

The unhappy woman fell on her knees, weeping.

"I adjure you," he continued solemnly, "you, my wife, Bertrande de Rolls, to swear now, here, on the crucifix, that I am an impostor and a cheat."

A crucifix was placed before Bertrande; she made a sign as if to push it away, endeavoured to speak, and feebly exclaimed, "No," then fell to the ground, and was carried out insensible.

This scene considerably shook the opinion of the magistrates. They could not believe that an impostor, whatever he might be, would have sufficient daring and presence of mind thus to turn into mockery all that was most sacred. They set a new inquiry on foot, which, instead of producing enlightenment, only plunged them into still greater obscurity. Out of thirty witnesses heard, more than three-quarters agreed in identifying as Martin Guerre the man who claimed his name. Never was greater perplexity caused by more extraordinary appearances. The remarkable resemblance upset all reasoning: some recognised him as Arnauld du Thill, and others asserted the exact contrary. He could hardly understand Basque, some said, though born in Biscay, was that astonishing, seeing he was only three when he left the country? He could neither wrestle nor fence well, but having no occasion to practise these exercises he might well have forgotten them. The shoemaker—who made his shoes afore-time, thought he took another measure, but he might have made a mistake before or be mistaken now. The prisoner further defended himself by recapitulating the circumstances of his first meeting with Bertrande, on his return, the thousand and one little details he had mentioned which he only could have known, also the letters in his possession, all of which could only be explained by the assumption that he was the veritable Martin Guerre. Was it likely that he would be wounded over the left eye and leg as the missing man was supposed to be? Was it likely that the old servant, that the four sisters, his uncle Pierre, many persons to whom he had related facts known only to himself, that all the community in short, would have recognised him? And even the very intrigue suspected by Bertrande, which had aroused her jealous anger, this very intrigue, if it really existed, was it not another proof of the verity of his claim, since the person concerned, as interested and as penetrating as the legitimate wife; had also accepted him as her former lover? Surely here was a mass of evidence sufficient to cast light on the case. Imagine an impostor arriving for the first time in a place where all the inhabitants are unknown to him, and attempting to personate a man who had dwelt there, who would have connections of all kinds, who would have played his part in a thousand different scenes, who would have confided his secrets, his opinions, to relations, friends, acquaintances, to all sorts of people; who had also a wife—that is to say, a person under whose eyes nearly his whole life would be passed, a person would study him perpetually, with whom he would be continually conversing on every sort of subject. Could such an impostor sustain his impersonation for a single day, without his memory playing him false? From the physical and moral impossibility of playing such a part, was it not reasonable to conclude that the accused, who had maintained it for more than two years, was the true Martin Guerre?

There seemed, in fact, to be nothing which could account for such an attempt being successfully made unless recourse was had to an accusation of sorcery. The idea of handing him over to the ecclesiastical authorities was briefly discussed, but proofs were necessary, and the judges hesitated. It is a principle of justice, which has become a precept in law, that in cases of uncertainty the accused has the benefit of the doubt; but at the period of which we are writing, these truths were far from being acknowledged; guilt was presumed rather than innocence; and torture, instituted to force confession from those who could not otherwise be convicted, is only explicable by supposing the judges convinced of the actual guilt of the accused; for no one would have thought of subjecting a possibly innocent person to this suffering. However, notwithstanding this prejudice, which has been handed down to us by some organs of the public ministry always disposed to assume the guilt of a suspected person,— notwithstanding this prejudice, the judges in this case neither ventured to condemn Martin Guerre themselves as an impostor, nor to demand the intervention of the Church. In this conflict of contrary testimony, which seemed to reveal the truth only to immediately obscure it again, in this chaos of arguments and conjectures which showed flashes of light only to extinguish them in greater darkness, consideration for the family prevailed. The sincerity of Bertrande, the future of the children, seemed reasons for proceeding with extreme caution, and this once admitted, could only yield to conclusive evidence. Consequently the Parliament adjourned the case, matters remaining in 'statu quo', pending a more exhaustive inquiry. Meanwhile, the accused, for whom several relations and friends gave surety, was allowed to be at liberty at Artigues, though remaining under careful surveillance.

Bertrande therefore again saw him an inmate of the house, as if no doubts had ever been cast on the legitimacy of their union. What thoughts passed through her mind during the long 'tete-a-tete'? She had accused this man of imposture, and now, notwithstanding her secret conviction, she was obliged to appear as if she had no suspicion, as if she had been mistaken, to humiliate herself before the impostor, and ask forgiveness for the insanity of her conduct; for, having publicly renounced her accusation by refusing to swear to it, she had no alternative left. In order to sustain her part and to save the honour of her children, she must treat this man as her husband and appear submissive and repentant; she must show him entire confidence, as the only means of rehabilitating him and lulling the vigilance of justice. What the widow of Martin Guerre must have suffered in this life of effort was a secret between God and herself, but she looked at her little daughter, she thought of her fast approaching confinement, and took courage.

One evening, towards nightfall, she was sitting near him in the most private corner of the garden, with her little child on her knee, whilst the adventurer, sunk in gloomy thoughts, absently stroked Sanxi's fair head. Both were silent, for at the bottom of their hearts each knew the other's thoughts, and, no longer able to talk familiarly, nor daring to appear estranged, they spent, when alone together, long hours of silent dreariness.

All at once a loud uproar broke the silence of their retreat; they heard the exclamations of many persons, cries of surprise mixed with angry tones, hasty footsteps, then the garden gate was flung violently open, and old Marguerite appeared, pale, gasping, almost breathless. Bertrande hastened towards her in astonishment, followed by her husband, but when near enough to speak she could only answer with inarticulate sounds, pointing with terror to the courtyard of the house. They looked in this direction, and saw a man standing at the threshold; they approached him. He stepped forward, as if to place himself between them. He was tall, dark; his clothes were torn; he had a wooden leg; his countenance was stern. He surveyed Bertrande with a gloomy look: she cried aloud, and fell back insensible; . . . she recognised her real husband!

Arnauld du Thill stood petrified. While Marguerite, distracted herself, endeavoured to revive her mistress, the neighbours, attracted by the noise, invaded the house, and stopped, gazing with stupefaction at this astonishing resemblance. The two men had the same features, the same height, the same bearing, and suggested one being in two persons. They gazed at each other in terror, and in that superstitious age the idea of sorcery and of infernal intervention naturally occurred to those present. All crossed themselves, expecting every moment to see fire from heaven strike one or other of the two men, or that the earth would engulf one of them. Nothing happened, however, except that both were promptly arrested, in order that the strange mystery might be cleared up.

The wearer of the wooden leg, interrogated by the judges, related that he came from Spain, where first the healing of his wound, and then the want of money, had detained him hitherto. He had travelled on foot, almost a beggar. He gave exactly the same reasons for leaving Artigues as had been given by the other Martin Guerre, namely, a domestic quarrel caused by jealous suspicion, the desire of seeing other countries, and an adventurous disposition. He had gone back to his birthplace, in Biscay; thence he entered the service of the Cardinal of Burgos; then the cardinal's brother had taken him to the war, and he had served with the Spanish troops; at the battle of St. Quentiny—his leg had been shattered by an arquebus ball. So far his recital was the counterpart of the one already heard by the judges from the other man. Now, they began to differ. Martin Guerre stated that he had been conveyed to a house by a man whose features he did not distinguish, that he thought he was dying, and that several hours elapsed of which he could give no account, being probably delirious; that he suffered later intolerable pain, and on coming to himself, found that his leg had been amputated. He remained long between life and death, but he was cared for by peasants who probably saved his life; his recovery was very slow. He discovered that in the interval between being struck down in the battle and recovering his senses, his papers had disappeared, but it was impossible to suspect the people who had nursed him with such generous kindness of theft. After his recovery, being absolutely destitute, he sought to return to France and again see his wife and child: he had endured all sorts of privations and fatigues, and at length, exhausted, but rejoicing at being near the end of his troubles, he arrived, suspecting nothing, at his own door. Then the terror of the old servant, a few broken words, made him guess at some misfortune, and the appearance of his wife and of a man so exactly like himself stupefied him. Matters had now been explained, and he only regretted that his wound had not at once ended his existence.

The whole story bore the impress of truth, but when the other prisoner was asked what he had to say he adhered to his first answers, maintaining their correctness, and again asserted that he was the real Martin Guerre, and that the new claimant could only be Arnauld du Thill, the clever impostor, who was said to resemble himself so much that the inhabitants of Sagias had agreed in mistaking him for the said Arnauld.

The two Martin Guerres were then confronted without changing the situation in the least; the first showing the same assurance, the same bold and confident bearing; while the second, calling on God and men to bear witness to his sincerity, deplored his misfortune in the most pathetic terms.

The judge's perplexity was great: the affair became more and more complicated, the question remained as difficult, as uncertain as ever. All the appearances and evidences were at variance; probability seemed to incline towards one, sympathy was more in favour of the other, but actual proof was still wanting.

At length a member of the Parliament, M. de Coras, proposed as a last chance before resorting to torture, that final means of examination in a barbarous age, that Bertrande should be placed between the two rivals, trusting, he said, that in such a case a woman's instinct would divine the truth. Consequently the two Martin Guerres were brought before the Parliament, and a few moments after Bertrande was led in, weak, pale, hardly able to stand, being worn out by suffering and advanced pregnancy. Her appearance excited compassion, and all watched anxiously to see what she would do. She looked at the two men, who had been placed at different ends of the hall, and turning from him who was nearest to her, went and knelt silently before the man with the wooden leg; then, joining her hands as if praying for mercy, she wept bitterly. So simple and touching an action roused the sympathy of all present; Arnauld du Thill grew pale, and everyone expected that Martin Guerre, rejoiced at being vindicated by this public acknowledgment, would raise his wife and embrace her. But he remained cold and stern, and in a contemptuous tone—

"Your tears, madame," he said; "they do not move me in the least, neither can you seek to excuse your credulity by the examples of my sisters and my uncle. A wife knows her husband more intimately than his other relations, as you prove by your present action, and if she is deceived it is because she consents to the deception. You are the sole cause of the misfortunes of my house, and to you only shall I ever impute them."

Thunderstruck by this reproach, the poor woman had no strength to reply, and was taken home more dead than alive.

The dignified language of this injured husband made another point in his favour. Much pity was felt for Bertrande, as being the victim of an audacious deception; but everybody agreed that thus it beseemed the real Martin Guerre to have spoken. After the ordeal gone through by the wife had been also essayed by the sisters and other relatives, who one and all followed Bertrande's example and accepted the new-comer, the court, having fully deliberated, passed the following sentence, which we transcribe literally:

"Having reviewed the trial of Arnauld du Thill or Pansette, calling himself Martin Guerre, a prisoner in the Conciergerie, who appeals from the decision of the judge of Rieux, etc.

"We declare that this court negatives the appeal and defence of the said Arnauld du Thill; and as punishment and amends for the imposture, deception, assumption of name and of person, adultery, rape, sacrilege, theft, larceny, and other deeds committed by the aforesaid du Thill, and causing the above-mentioned trial; this court has condemned and condemns him to do penance before the church of Artigue, kneeling, clad in his shirt only, bareheaded and barefoot, a halter on his neck, and a burning torch in his hand, and there he shall ask pardon from God, from the King, and from justice, from the said Martin Guerre and Bertrande de Rolls, husband and wife: and this done, the aforesaid du Thill shall be delivered into the hands of the executioners of the King's justice, who shall lead him through the customary streets and crossroads of the aforesaid place of Artigues, and, the halter on his neck, shall bring him before the house of the aforesaid Martin Guerre, where he shall be hung and strangled upon a gibbet erected for this purpose, after which his body shall be burnt: and for various reasons and considerations thereunto moving the court, it has awarded and awards the goods of the aforesaid Arnauld du Thill, apart from the expenses of justice, to the daughter born unto him by the aforesaid Bertrande de Rolls, under pretence of marriage falsely asserted by him, having thereto assumed the name and person of the aforesaid Martin Guerre, by this mans deceiving the aforesaid de Rolls; and moreover the court has exempted and exempts from this trial the aforesaid Martin Guerre and Bertrande de Rolls, also the said Pierre Guerre, uncle of the aforesaid Martin, and has remitted and remits the aforesaid Arnauld du Thill to the aforesaid judge of Rieux, in order that the present sentence may be executed according to its form and tenor. Pronounced judicially this 12th day of September 1560."

This sentence substituted the gallows for the decapitation decreed by the first judge, inasmuch as the latter punishment was reserved for criminals of noble birth, while hanging was inflicted on meaner persons.

When once his fate was decided, Arnauld du Thill lost all his audacity. Sent back to Artigues, he was interrogated in prison by the judge of Rieux, and confessed his imposture at great length. He said the idea first occurred to him when, having returned from the camp in Picardy, he was addressed as Martin Guerre by several intimate friends of the latter. He then inquired as to the sort of life, the habits and relations of, this man, and having contrived to be near him, had watched him closely during the battle. He saw him fall, carried him away, and then, as the reader has already seen, excited his delirium to the utmost in order to obtain possession of his secrets. Having thus explained his successful imposture by natural causes, which excluded any idea of magic or sorcery, he protested his penitence, implored the mercy of God, and prepared himself for execution as became a Christian.

The next day, while the populace, collecting from the whole neighbourhood, had assembled before the parish church of Artigues in order to behold the penance of the criminal, who, barefoot, attired in a shirt, and holding a lighted torch in his hand, knelt at the entrance of the church, another scene, no less painful, took place in the house of Martin Guerre. Exhausted by her suffering, which had caused a premature confinement, Bertrande lay on her couch of pain, and besought pardon from him whom she had innocently wronged, entreating him also to pray for her soul. Martin Guerre, sitting at her bedside, extended his hand and blessed her. She took his hand and held it to her lips; she could no longer speak. All at once a loud noise was heard outside: the guilty man had just been executed in front of the house. When finally attached to the gallows, he uttered a terrible cry, which was answered by another from inside the house. The same evening, while the body of the malefactor was being consumed by fire, the remains of a mother and child were laid to rest in consecrated ground.

www.ingramcontent.com/pod-product-compliance
Lightning Source LLC
Chambersburg PA
CBHW022121090426
42743CB00008B/950